called to be

devotions
by teens for teens

CONCORDIA PUBLISHING HOUSE · SAINT LOUIS

Dedicated
to
any
teenager
who
ever
used
the
phone

(contents

Introduction

"So glad you called!"

My immediate question is who is calling and who is on the other end of the call?

If the caller is me, then it's God who is glad I called Him. "Call upon Me in the day of trouble," He says (Psalm 50:15). "Cast all your anxiety on Him because He cares for you" (1 Peter 5:7). So, God issues His invitation and hopes we will call Him up. He wants to hear from us; He wants to help; He wants to join our celebrations. And He is glad when we call.

If God is the caller, then it is we who are glad He called. He calls us by name (Isaiah 43:1). He calls us to follow (Luke 9:23). He calls on us to call on Him. And we're glad because we know we are part of His family—loved, forgiven, restored.

The teens who wrote these devotions have a neat perspective on all this calling (perhaps because they spend so much time on the phone). They know God; they know His promises. They know His guidance and expectations.

They know His grace and forgiveness. They have the spirit, humor, and enthusiasm of youth. And they have keen spiritual insights to share with their peers.

The teens who read these devotions will be glad they paid a call on the writers and they will be blessed by God's Spirit through the words of these young authors.

Terry Dittmer

Associate Director, Youth Ministry
The Lutheran Church—Missouri Synod

A Talented Display
of Christianity

Michelle Belviy

Read: John 15:1

"Touchdown!" the crowd cheered as the star quarterback, Joey, made the final touchdown at the buzzer. "Wildcats 23, Bears 17," proclaimed the announcer over the intercom. The crowd watched as the entire Wildcats football team hoisted Joey on their shoulders and carried him around.

Yes, that was the life of Joey Steinbeck. He had many friends, a normal family life, and a basically planned football career that was set up by coaches and scouts. Many would say that Joey had it made, but no one knew that he was really miserable. It wasn't that he was ungrateful. Money may have been tight for his family, but he was content. And he had a lot of friends. His career in football was as good as his grades in school—straight A's all the way. He just didn't know why he felt as if something was missing in his life.

One day, while Joey was changing in the locker room after practice, he noticed one of his friends, Paul, putting on a chain with a symbol on it. Joey had remembered his grandmother showing him that symbol when he was younger. She used to tell him of a man named Jesus who performed great miracles. Joey thought they were just stories, but he went over to Paul and asked him where he had gotten the chain. Paul explained what the symbol meant. Paul told him that Jesus died to save us from our sins and what Jesus meant to him in his life. Paul asked Joey if he wanted to go to church with him on Sunday to hear more.

Sunday came, and Joey was a little nervous. He kept thinking, "What if they don't like me?" This kept running through his mind as he got dressed. Paul showed up just as Joey was putting on his shoes. He thought, "Here goes nothing," as he hopped into Paul's car and took off.

When they pulled up at the church, Joey looked at the size and colors of the stained-glass windows. Inside, Paul introduced him to some people, one of whom was a cute girl named Kira. "Maybe I'll like it here after all," Joey laughed to himself. The service was starting, so Paul, Joey, and Kira all sat down in a pew together. Joey listened to the sermon and the Bible reading, John 15:1–8. Something was very different about this place. After the service, the three new friends talked for hours about Christ, the church, about life …

Joey still plays like a champion, but now he plays with Spirit. He goes to church regularly and has started to get his family to go as well. He thanks God for his good friend Paul every day. Paul helped Joey to see that talents can come in many forms such as sports or witnessing to others. Joey also learned that Christ is the key.

Pray: Dear heavenly Father, thank You for all the talents You have given to us. Be with us as we learn how to use our talents to give You honor. Help us to be stronger witnesses and use our talents to help bring people closer to You, by the power of the Holy Spirit. Amen.

A New Family

Kendra Borglum

Read: John 14:18

Baptism is our birth into new life, a life filled with the love of our Father. A new family is ours, for we are now children of God. It doesn't matter what age you are in this life. When you get baptized, you are only a child in God's eyes. In the family of Christ, you age not by how many years you have lived, but by how God knows you. He is your Father. He gives us commandments and rules to live by. He gives us His love and care. He even gave us His only Son, Jesus, to die for our sins. What a wonderful Father! This new family we belong to is filled with love, joy, and honesty. This family will last for all of eternity.

God our Father will not abandon us as orphans, He will come to us. He lives with us and in us. He teaches us what we need to know to prepare for the future.

The apostle Paul uses adoption to illustrate the believer's new relationship with God. In

Roman culture, the adopted person lost all rights in his old family and gained all the rights of a legitimate child in his new family. He became a full heir to his father's estate. Likewise, when a person becomes a Christian, he or she gains all the privileges and responsibilities of a child in God's family. One of these outstanding privileges is being led by the Holy Spirit. (See Galatians 4:5–6.)

Pray: Dear Father, thank You for adopting us into Your family. Help me to spread Your Word and wisdom to everyone I see. Let me know I can call on You in my time of need, and remind me of that even when things are going right. You are the best Father anyone could ask for. Amen.

Jesus Loves Me

(Matthew Bruning)

Read: Psalm 98:1–4

Everyone knows the words to "Jesus Loves Me, This I Know," but have you ever sat down and looked at what those simple words mean? Have you ever thought that a common children's song could really be a summary of everything that makes you a child of God?

The first line, "Jesus loves me, this I know," is the simplest, yet possibly the strongest proclamation of faith. The fact that you *know* that Jesus loves you is so comforting. It is not that you think or that there is any doubt, but that, unquestionably, you *know* He loves you. Jesus loves us even though we are all filled with sin. No matter what we do, Jesus loves us—He died to save us. The next line, "For the Bible tells me so," shows that we believe God's Word and put our faith in what it tells us.

The second part of the stanza, "Little ones to Him belong; They are weak, but He is strong," shows that no matter who you are, no matter what your age, you are a child of God. All of us are weak and can do nothing without the help of Jesus. As the psalmist writes in Psalm 18:2, "The LORD is my rock, my fortress and my deliverer." He is the firm foundation that we must use as support in our lives. We by ourselves are unable to do anything without putting our total trust in Jesus Christ.

The refrain is my personal favorite. "Yes, Jesus loves me, Yes, Jesus loves me." Yes, Jesus does love each of us. What more needs to be said?

Pray: Most loving Father, help me to remember the meaning of this song and the other wonderful songs that glorify Your name. Never let the singing of Your wonderful love stop. In Your joyous name. Amen.

There Is a Reason

Read: Ecclesiastes 3:1

Football season was always a busy time for Jason, especially in his junior year. With practices, games, classes, and homework, Jason did not have much time for anything else. Since football practices took up most of his time during the week, Jason stayed home from church on Sunday to do homework.

Four games into the football season, Jason broke his arm. He had been having a really good year playing defense, but the break ended his football season. He, of course, thought that no good could possibly come from this injury.

The next Sunday, Jason asked his pastor if he could talk to him. He asked him why God would let something like that happen to him. His pastor replied that God did not cause the injury to punish Jason, but that maybe it had happened so he could get his priorities straight. Jason's pastor noted that now he could become more involved in the church and youth group or perhaps in helping others in some way. The pastor reminded Jason of God's promise that all things—even those that look bad to us—work together for good for those who love God. When Jesus was crucified it didn't look good, but look how it turned out—Jesus paid for our sins on the cross.

Jason thought it over and realized that his injury would allow him to put God first and enable him to help others. After all, there was next year—and things would be different.

Pray: Dear heavenly Father, let me never forget that You are most important in my life. Help me keep my priorities straight. In Your all-powerful name. Amen.

I Was Hungry

(Joshua Dehnke)

Read: Matthew 25:35–40

Hmmm ... I like fettucini Alfredo ... but I haven't had manicotti in ages, ... and linguine sounds delicious, I thought, studying the menu at my favorite Italian restaurant. With so many choices, how could I decide?

Suddenly, a different thought popped into my head: What if I had *no* choices and finished dinner still famished?

I like to eat. My friends will attest to that. My parents could show a long supermarket receipt as proof. Sometimes complete strangers ask me how I can eat so much. I tell them I have a very fast metabolism or that I'm just a growing boy. Leftovers? Not in our house. Seconds? Of course. Full? Not likely.

However, on this particular evening I thought about how many others would go to bed on an empty stomach—in my hometown of St. Louis, in America, or in the world!

How often do I actually think about world hunger, and, when I do, how real is it to me? After all, *those* people live miles away, and I only see them on television. I do not give to the hungry, but does it matter? Feeding one person for one meal is insignificant.

Jesus disagrees: "I was hungry and you gave Me something to eat. ... I tell you the truth, whatever you did for one of the least of these brothers of Mine, you did for Me" (Matthew 25:35–40).

It doesn't matter who or how many I could feed, or how much I could feed them. When I feed the hungry in any small way, it is service to the Lord. Through my offerings at church, helping with food drives, or praying for the hungry, I can do something small to help with a big problem.

Pray: Lord Jesus, help me to see the pains of those around me and throughout the world. Remind me of Your unconditional love that caused You to give Your life, even for me. Help me to share that love with all I can touch, near and far. In Your name. Amen.

Temple of the Spirit

Read: 1 Corinthians 6:19–20

Joshua Dehnke

The Beatles were the hottest band. People bought record albums, not compact discs. Miniskirts, bell-bottoms, and knee-high boots were fashionable for the *first* time. Personal computers didn't exist. The only computers were as large as the room they were kept in. No one had heard of microwave ovens, Michael Jordan, cellular phones, or STDs.

This is what life was like in the '60s. Clothing, music, and technology were different, as were the problems facing society. The main danger from having sex before marriage was pregnancy. Today, STD, which stands for sexually transmitted disease, is one of the most feared acronyms across the globe.

Although the law against all types of idolatry was given thousands of years ago to Moses, many people today still need convincing that idolatry is sinful.

The apostle Paul prescribes a unique outlook: "Do you not know that your body is a temple of the Holy Spirit, who is in you, whom you have received from God? You are not your own; you were bought at a price. Therefore honor God with your body" (1 Corinthians 6:19–20).

That price for which we were bought was Jesus' blood shed on the cross—a high price to pay for our sinful selves. Our bodies are gifts from God—more complex and beautiful than anything in the world. Our bodies are home for the Holy Spirit—a temple! We should do all we can to take care of this precious gift so we can better honor God through witness and service to others.

Pray: Lord Jesus, thank You for Your sacrifice on the cross. Remind us of the pain You suffered to save us from ourselves. Help us to treat our bodies with respect and care so we may honor You with our praise and actions. Amen.

Responsibility

Read: 1 Corinthians 6:19-20

"Make good choices! Be careful!" My mom yells these words as I leave for the evening. I was raised to make good choices. Now that I am a teenager, I have a lot of new freedom, and with this new freedom comes new responsibilities.

I have to know *before* I go out what I will allow to go in my body or what I will choose to happen to my body. I can't decide when I'm asked because I know the heat of the moment could get to me. So how about a beer? a cigarette? a kiss? a little more than a kiss? sex? What am I going to say? *Sure, I only live once* or *I only live once, why ruin it early?* I have come to realize that these things could rip my life apart.

I like to think of my body as a rental car. God has loaned me this car; my life is the journey I'm going on. This car serves many purposes: to have fun in, go places in, take care of, and eventually return. It needs tune-ups and repairs, oil changes and gas. This car needs to be kept in good shape. I would try never to run it into something or drive irresponsibly. I wouldn't give in to someone who wanted to drive or take advantage of my "new wheels."

Each of these things can relate to the responsibilities I have for my body. I have to tune up my faith. Put oil in my lamp and keep it burnin'. I shouldn't put anything harmful in my body or abuse it. I am to practice self-control and not "run in to something." This body I have is borrowed to do the work God wants me to do. I have no right to ruin it.

I need to be prepared to say no. I once heard someone say, "I don't have a lot of peer pressure, just a lot of friends who drink." Peer pressure isn't someone saying, "Everyone is doing it." It's being around everyone who is doing it.

God has given us our bodies, and we are to take care of them. It's not an option, it's a responsibility. 1 Corinthians 6:19–20 says, "Do you not know that your body is a temple of the Holy Spirit, who is in you, whom you have received from God? You are not your own; you were bought at a price. Therefore honor God with your body." And we read in 1 Peter 2:24, "He Himself bore our sins in His body on the tree, so that we might die to sins and live for righteousness." Christ paid for your sins with His body because He loves you. So respect *your* body—it is the work of the Lord!

Pray: Dear heavenly Father, thank You for our beautiful bodies. Help us to be responsible and take care of them. Thank You for sacrificing Your Son for us. Help us to make decisions that are positive for temples of Your Spirit. Remind us that we must use our bodies to work for You. Fill us with Your love and life. Amen.

Parents

Erin Dittmer

Read: Proverbs 17:6

"Mom, are you wearing that?!" Lauren asked as they were leaving for dinner. The outfit wasn't that bad ... for the mom on *The Brady Bunch!* Lauren, on the other hand, was wearing something stylish.

I guess we have all had those days when one of our parents pulls out those bell-bottom pants or sings "Yakety Yak" to us. And it's really embarrassing, I know. I have two parents who still haven't gotten the fact that we are living in the '90s. We need to understand that they probably went through the same things with their parents. It's because we are from different generations. Your mom may like her polyester pants while you prefer your jeans. These things are easy to deal with. It can't be *that* bad to adjust to different style preferences. It's like accepting different personalities at church and school.

But how about priorities, morals, that kind of stuff? I'm sure you have disagreements on "teen issues." My parents used to be big on the dating topic. Was 15 too young? Should I wait until I am 30? Or, how about your choice of friends? Do your parents ask you about their families and lifestyles?

It may seem annoying, but you need to accept that they have been through it all. They aren't brain-dead. They love you and care about you. Listen to their advice and be patient with them. They are only concerned about you. Can you imagine what it would be like if your parents didn't give a rip about where you go and whom you date? We really do need them. A lot of things have changed over the years, but many of the problems we go through now were there 20 years ago. So they understand.

Our parents' styles may be different and their opinions may be opposite ours, but we are all here now, together. We are all children of God. No matter how diverse we are, we have that in common—God loves us and gave His Son to die for us. That *never* changes.

Pray: Father, thank You for the gift of parents. Help me to listen to my parents and to respect them even when I disagree with them or when they embarrass me. In Jesus' name. Amen.

The Pressure's On

Read: 1 Corinthians 10:13

Imagine a girl. She's pretty popular and outgoing, known as a Christian with good values. This girl is a good student who rarely does anything wrong. Meet Anna.

Like most teenagers, Anna deals with peer pressure, but in the past it wasn't even an issue. It was simple. She wouldn't give in. Then, things went downhill. Anna's home life was not going well. She feared that her family was being split apart. Anna was going through hard times; concern for her family was distracting her from her school work. Even though her friends tried to help, Anna ignored them and started hanging with a different crowd. For awhile these new "friends" invited Anna to parties where drugs and alcohol were available. She always refused.

One Saturday night Anna's parents were fighting over the usual pointless issues. Anna knew she had to "get out" and fast. A friend called and invited Anna to a party. This time to everyone's surprise, Anna decided to go.

Next you would probably expect to hear that Anna gave in to pressures at the party, but you would be mistaken. When she arrived, she saw what was going on and did not like it. Anna wondered if she should leave or stay. She asked God for help and strength. As she looked around, she saw a "real" friend from her old crowd who was at the party. The two realized they were not alone. They had each other to help and most important, they had God. What would you do?

Pray: Lord, no matter how strong the pressure is, help me to resist and to turn to You in times of need. Strengthen me through Your Holy Spirit and help me to remember all You have done for me—especially Your suffering on the cross—that I am Your forgiven child. Thanks for Your love. Amen.

A Way Out

Read: Romans 8:35

(Erica Eden)

It's 11:30 P.M. and you can't sleep. There just isn't enough time for everything, is there? Finals, work, homework, club meetings, and of course practice. You're stressed!

It's hard to find time to do all that you have planned in a 24-hour day. Don't forget that you have to sleep. For a teenager, life can get pretty stressful. You need a break, someone to talk to. Unfortunately, you don't know whom to talk to or just what to do about your situation. Don't count God out. He is our peace. Romans 5:1–2 says, "Therefore, since we have been justified through faith, we have peace with God through our Lord Jesus Christ, through whom we have gained access by faith into this grace in which we now stand. And we rejoice in the hope of the glory of God." Never let any job, sports game, or friend keep you from spending time with God and seeking that peace. God, who loves you, died for you, and forgives you, will surely help you.

Any time you've got too much stress in your life, turn to God. He cares so much for you and is always ready to listen to your problems. Don't stress. God is there for you. Just talk to Him. Believe it! He wants to hear what's going on in your life, and He will help. So, any time you find yourself in a stressful situation, just talk to God. He's listening.

Pray: Father, being a teenager isn't always easy. Sometimes I take on too many things and leave You out, God, but You still love me and are there for me. Please help me through those tough times and help me always find my way back to You. In Jesus' name. Amen.

The Greatest Servant Event of All

Read: 1 Corinthians 6:20

(Doug Fiehler)

One Christmas morning a little boy began opening his presents. He ripped off the wrapping paper, peered inside, gave it a little attention, then ripped into the next present. To him it was Christmastime, a time to receive presents and enjoy them.

He thought that the stack of presents would never run out. The pile grew smaller and smaller with each opened present. He was very happy … until he looked up and saw no more presents.

The tears welled up in his eyes and he began sobbing. He threw a tantrum and laid there moaning on the carpet. His mother picked him up and put him on the sofa next to her and said, "I was so happy to be giving you all of these presents, and you were happy to receive them. Then when you ran out, you became upset. Son, it is more blessed to give than to receive."

Two thousand years ago we were given the greatest gift of all. Jesus Christ came to relieve us of the burden of our sins. He showed His love to all people. This was the greatest servant event of all.

As the son in the story, we were enjoying all of the gifts our Father had given us, but not all in the way they were intended because of our sinful nature. He came, saved us, and showed us His ceaseless love.

He also commanded us to "go and make disciples of all nations" (Matthew 28:19). He wants us to spread His Word and love to all people. What better way to do this than by serving others?

Pray: Lord, thank You for the greatest servant event of all time. Help me to be a servant to others and to You. In Jesus' name. Amen.

A Choice

Read: Colossians 2:20–23

"Wanna come over tonight?"

"Sure."

A short time later …

"Where is your family?"

"They're gone for the night."

"Oh, … what's with the candles?"

"Atmosphere … so we can get to know each other *much* better!"

"Well, you obviously don't know me as well as you think you do. I'm not that kind of person! I'm *not* that easy! I'm leaving!"

This is a temptation for people of both sexes. Emotions and hormones run wild, and control can be difficult. Sometimes the conscience checks in; sometimes it's suppressed. Sometimes a reaction is ready, sometimes it's held back to protect your image, sometimes the reaction is not ready or even thought of.

God frowns on premarital sex. He loves us very much and made this one of His laws to prevent us from injuring ourselves, others, and our relationships. Sexual intercourse should be reserved for marriage.

We should not only agree with God's law but should embrace it and make it part of our lives. We should be ready to react positively when the situation arises. We need to be bold and confident when we make our stand. God gave us our conscience; we should listen to it. The situation needs to stay under control, God's control. So take a minute right now to think of what you're going to say when you're tempted. Jesus was prepared when the devil tempted Him (see Matthew 4). He was faithful to His calling, even to the point of dying for our sins—even the times we didn't resist. Remember that and ask for His help in resisting temptations.

Pray: Dear Lord, I thank You for giving me my own free will. Give me Your strength to make good decisions in my life and to stand up for them. Watch over me and guide me. In Jesus' name I pray. Amen.

We're Free! Now What?

Read: Galatians 5:13

"You, my brothers, were called to be free" (Galatians 5:13). How do we respond to this call? As Christians we have all been set free and now live our lives with this gift of freedom. But what exactly have we been set free from, and how should we now live our lives in respect to this gift of freedom?

First, we are cleansed and thereby free of our sins through Christ's death and resurrection. That sentence covers such a large concept that we as humans cannot fully understand its magnitude. We sin every day and have been sinning every day and will continue to sin as long as we live. That adds up to a lot of sin. We all commit so many sins each day that we can't possibly count them. And yet, one man, Jesus, paid the price for every one of these sins in one ultimate act of love toward us—His gruesome death and glorious resurrection.

So, you say, great! End of story. Right?

Wrong! If you read the end of Galatians 5:13, you see that it says, "But do not use your freedom to indulge in the sinful nature; rather, serve one another in love." It's as though someone gave you the most expensive gift of the highest quality that you will ever receive. And the best part of it all is that all He requests of you is to bestow the same gift of love to others! You respond to Him, not because He'll refuse to give you the gift if you don't follow His command perfectly, but because you realize the magnitude of His love and grace. All you want to do is try to live your life in Him.

We are all sinners, but our many sins have been covered through Jesus' death and resurrection. We live with this joyful news in our hearts, showing happiness and gratitude to those we encounter in our daily lives. Praise God!

Pray: Lord, thank You for setting us free through Your death and resurrection. Help me to share Your act of love with others. In Jesus' name. Amen.

It Was Lust at First Sight!

(Luke Hennings

Read: 1 Corinthians 13

There's love, and then there's lust. Their meanings are very different, yet they are often confused as one and the same. Why does this happen? Why is it important that we be able to tell them apart? Lust and love are both feelings directed toward others. They both make you feel good. If both make you feel good, why do we need to tell the difference? The answer is very straightforward: God commands us to love, not to lust.

Here's the big difference between lust and love: Love is a feeling that wants to build another person up. It is built around compassion, patience, selflessness, and the desire to make the other person's life as joyful as possible. To see true love, you only need to look at Jesus. Through love He served us, sacrificed for us, and died for us so we could be forgiven and love and serve Him. *That* is perfect love.

Lust wishes only to please itself and has no real concern about the other person. It may be based on the looks of a person, or his or her social status, and often has the tendency to be spontaneous (one day you may feel really attracted toward this person, the next day you've forgotten he or she is alive). If you're wondering to yourself, "Oh my! Maybe I lust after this person and don't love him or her." I offer a note of clarification: It's possible to think someone looks good and still love that person. Just try to make sure that's not the only reason you love him or her. If you're still confused, there's a "lovely" chapter in 1 Corinthians (chapter 13) that lists the qualities of love. Why not use it as a checklist to see if you really do love this person?

One final note: Every person lusts, but how many people really love? Love is a response that takes effort and commitment to exist, where lust is more a spur of the moment "Wow, he or she looks good" type of reaction. So with God's help try to take the time and put forth the effort to respond to our Lord's call to love.

Pray: Dear Lord, thank You for the guidance of Your Word. Help me to turn to You for strength and wisdom. Amen.

Popularity

Read: Psalm 7:3–12; 73:16–19

It's tougher than ever to grow up with good strong Christian values. As teens we are bombarded daily by things that tempt us to live in an ungodly fashion. TV, movies, and music are constantly hitting us with immoral messages. At school, we are tempted by friends (or even those who are not our friends) to stray. Alcohol and drugs are readily available to most of us if we want them. Violence among teens is on the rise. High schoolers are having premarital intercourse more and more. This is leading to higher pregnancy rates, abortions, and STDs. All of these activities are wrong, yet these are some of the most popular forms of "recreation" among teens today.

It seems that people who don't follow the Lord's commands get to have all the fun. (See Psalm 7:3–12.) It may seem that way while we're on earth, but it won't last forever. Those who depend on the grace of God and believe in Christ as Lord and Savior by the power of the Holy Spirit will receive their reward in heaven. Those who do not believe in Jesus will also receive *their* reward on that final Judgment Day. (See Psalm 73:16–19.) Since we are saved by God's grace, we want to obey His will and turn away from sin and trust in God's will for our lives. I don't know about you, but I would rather follow God than disobey Him.

Pray: Dear Lord, help me to remain true to Your Word. Help me to resist the temptations here on earth. Continue to remind me that my reward will be eternity in heaven with You. In Jesus' name. Amen.

The Future

(Jennifer Griebel)

Read: Isaiah 65:17–25

Have you ever listened to those predictions about the end of the world? You know—global warming, huge meteorites, devastating earthquakes, the list goes on and on. Some of the things people say seem very real and believable, even scary, but in Isaiah the Bible tells us that God will destroy the world and then create a new heaven and earth for all believers. It sometimes seems the future of the world will be bad and scary—can you imagine what people thought on the first Good Friday? But God promises that the new heaven and new earth will be without sadness. There will be happiness for believers. What must have seemed terrible on Good Friday turned out better than anyone could have imagined—Jesus paid for our sins.

Sometimes we think there is no future for us, no reason for us to continue. Someone may die in the family, or you might study very hard for a test and still get a bad grade. Life sometimes doesn't seem fair. Other times we are afraid and unsure of our futures. These uncertainties can frighten us. We have to be strong in Christ and remember that God will never leave us and that He has plans for our lives.

When we are scared, we need to think about the footprints in the sand to see how God carried us in times of trouble. He is always there for us through the good times and the bad. Look back and see where He has carried you in the past. See how He will be with you in the future.

Pray: Dear heavenly Father, when we feel that our futures are uncertain, help us know that You are always with us and have plans for our future. Amen.

Power of Perseverance

Andy Harrigan

Read: Psalm 57:1

Every year natural disasters make victims out of millions of people all over the world. Most of these victims, obviously, don't feel gladdened by the fact that their home or livelihood has been destroyed by something beyond their control. This was not the case with Terrel. His home was destroyed by a tornado.

When Terrel's home was destroyed, he did not feel gladdened, but he reacted differently than most people. He did not even see himself as unlucky. Rather than feeling sorry for himself, Terrel picked himself up and prayed to God, thankful that he was alive and well. I know more than a few people would have lost hope and put their worldly possessions in front of their love for God. Terrel saw the circumstances as a test of faith. God saw in Terrel a person who was very strong in his faith. Most important, He saw a person who would not back down from a challenge.

God tests us in many ways. Why would Terrel feel so blessed to be tested with such severity? Well, after thinking about it, I guess it does seem severe. God challenges us to look more closely at Him. I believe, as Terrel did, that God will never test me beyond endurance. God has the power to overcome anything that I encounter. In fact, He overcame sin and death by dying on the cross. I need to lean on my risen Savior for all my needs.

Pray: Father in heaven, let me never stray from Your arms. Let me take refuge under Your wings. And with Your Word, I will have the power to outlast all that stands in my way. Thank You for calling me on this special day. Amen.

Tools of the Trade

(Andy Harrigan)

Read: Matthew 25:40

On the first morning of the servant event, I sat in the cafeteria after breakfast where about a hundred other ready-to-work youth anxiously awaited deployment to our work sites. In the doorway, a stocky middle-aged man stood. He introduced himself as Greg, the person in charge of the work projects. Greg remained standing in the doorway with a basketball under his right arm and a hammer in his belt. Standing there, silent in his denim overalls, Greg had a very blunt way of presenting himself. We listened as if waiting for a speech or special presentation.

Finally Greg asked, "Any basketball players in the room?" A few people hesitantly raised their hands. Greg chose a volunteer, Angie, and tossed the basketball to her as he continued, "This is the most important tool you may use all week."

I looked around the room, noticing heads turning with inquiring looks. Greg went on to say, "God created each of us differently. These differences should not hinder a person but should help a person to achieve goals and to accomplish tasks. People have different strengths, and only those who see differences as limitations manage to limit their abilities.

"Jesus said He came into the world to serve, not to be served. He served us by willingly paying for our sins on the cross. Because of His service, there are many ways we can serve one another. Some of us can pound a nail into a piece of wood, others can help someone with a jump shot. You will be a servant and a witness to God this week. If it is not through pounding a nail, then it may be through spending time with a child in the neighborhood or helping an elderly person cross the street."

How will you serve God today?

Pray: Father in heaven, grant me the strength to be of service to You in all that I do. Help me to walk in Your ways with all the tools You have given me. On this day I am very proud to have been called. I ask this in Jesus' name. Amen.

Suicide

Read: Jeremiah 29:11-13

Jill seemed to have a perfect life. She was popular, drove a great car, had great parents, and basically got along with everyone. The whole school was shocked one Sunday night when Jill tried to kill herself.

As strange as this may sound, it happens more often than we'd like to think. I've read results of a national survey that state that about 24 percent of teenage girls consider suicide in a given year. Many of these people attempt suicide and some complete their suicide attempts. (Guys also attempt suicide.) These people feel overwhelmed by life. They think that life is meaningless, that they aren't pretty enough, nobody loves them, or that they never do anything right. God doesn't think so! He has plans for all people. (See Jeremiah 29:11-13.)

If you know of anyone who is feeling this way, try to help him or her. Tell her how much she means to you. Tell him how much he means to God. Help her get some counseling. Who knows? One day you could be so hurt that you feel that life isn't worth living. It is! God gives us a chance. He isn't finished with us yet! God can and will help us, all of us, in rough times. He loves us so much He gave His Son for our sins and raises us to life through faith.

Pray: Dear Lord, remind me that You have plans for me. Keep showing me that my life is not a waste. I know my reward will be great in heaven. Help me stick out the pain and keep my faith in You. In Jesus' name. Amen.

Did You Know?

Jake Hower

Read: 1 Corinthians 9:24–27

Did you know that you are an athlete? You are. You are an athlete competing in the greatest race of a lifetime, your lifetime!

The thing about the course is that it's a lot tougher than it looks. In fact, it's almost like an obstacle course. The path has many traps and snares along the way that are designed to trip you up. What stinks is that you can't see most of them till the damage is done.

Your competitor, the master player, knows every inch of the entire course. He is especially familiar with those traps that inflict the most harm. Like the competitor he is, he loves to exploit your weaknesses. To him there are no rules. And he will cheat to win.

Now for the good news. You have the greatest coach that you could ever desire. He is the only one who ever won this race on His own. Not only did He win, He ran the course perfectly. By dying for our sins and rising again, He won for us the crown of life. This coach will pick you up when you fall. He will show you the best path to take. He will even give you those little nudges when you need them the most. He has even supplied you with the ultimate training manual, the Bible. He is all that you need to win this race. Trust in Him; He won't ever steer you wrong. Remember, the race has already started, so get going!

Pray: Lord, give me the strength to run the race as best I can, and grant me the endurance to gain the prize. Thank You, Lord, for showing me the way. Help me to follow Your example. Amen.

Beer Goggles Make It Hard to See God

Read: Ephesians 5:17–18

Hey, do you want a beer?

Simple question, isn't it? It wasn't a demand. There was no "do it, or else" threat behind it. It was merely a question. What is the general response the majority of the time? "Sure!"

What is the big deal? So what? I mean, what's wrong with having a drink? Well, let me rephrase the question. How often does it stop at just *a* drink? Rarely, if ever. Now we aren't just violating the law, we're violating good sense.

"So now you're saying there is something wrong with getting drunk?!"

Well … yeah, I am.

Listen. God gave each of us a brain and the ability to use it. Let's face it, there aren't too many intellectual drunks out there. Most of them have difficulty finding their keys or even their pockets for that matter. Do you really think that is what God had in mind for you when He sent

Jesus to the cross for your sins? Of course it isn't. (See Romans 6:1–2.) He loves you, but how can He reveal His plan to you if you're intoxicated, passed out, or even worse? You or someone close to you could end up dead. It happens. So instead of using your hands to hold drinks, try folding them in prayer. I guarantee you'll feel better in the morning.

Pray: Lord, fill me with Your Spirit. Grant me understanding that I may see what Your will is for my life, the courage to follow it, and forgiveness when I fail. Amen.

Consume Mass Quantities

Read: Psalm 23

Josh Hower

King Heroin is my shepherd,
I shall always want,
He maketh me lie down in the gutters
He leadeth me beside troubled waters
He destroyeth my soul.

—Author Unknown

Who is your shepherd? Whom do you follow? How do you spend your extra money, your free time? What thoughts most frequently run through your head? For the person in the poem, it was heroin. For a year and a half of my life it was alcohol.

Through my sophomore summer and junior year, beer might as well have been one of the four major food groups. "Consume Mass Quantities" was the catch phrase, and consume we did. If you are worn out from living two lives and from the lies that supposedly hold your life together, open your heart to God and show Him your guts. He will offer you a way out and He promises to be with you every step of the way. (See Deuteronomy 31:8.)

Alcohol is no longer my shepherd—Jesus is. He is ready to provide for you too. He walked into the valley of death and laid down His life for you. There will always be something wanting to take control of my life. Drugs hinder your perception of reality. Be sure that the devil will find the "drug" that works for you, be it money, pleasure, happiness, or heroin. Do not let it destroy your soul so instead we might together "dwell in the house of the Lord forever."

Pray: Lord, we come to You as sinners. We are sheep who are easily led astray. Help us to realize our weaknesses and lay them at Your feet saying, "Here, help me." Lord, may we always be intoxicated by Your love and realize no sin is too great to be covered by the saving blood of Your Son. Amen.

Hunger Pains

Read: Matthew 25:31–46

"Uncle, uncle, uncle, ... please, uncle, ... hungry ... uncle ... uncle?"

Close your eyes and imagine a child barely clothed and so skinny you see the bones in his face. See the dirt under his nails and in his hair, see the agony of hopelessness in his eyes. He tugs on your pant leg, begging you for anything, following you for blocks at a time. See him crying out in any English word he knows to get your attention. You have to stop! "Uncle, uncle, uncle, ... please, uncle, ... hungry ... uncle ... uncle?"

After five months in India last year, I learned one thing. *We as Christians are blessed beyond what we deserve.* Children starve from malnutrition while we take food for granted—something that will always be there. If you could feed the whole world till there was not a hungry soul, would you do it?

We can. (See John 6:35.) The world as a whole is starving, and we as Christians are blessed beyond what we deserve. Are we taking our faith for granted, the gift of the "bread of life"? Look at the world, look at the United States—do you see the agony and the hopelessness? Do you see a search for meaning and a search to be fulfilled? Do you see them crying out through the media, clothing, and music lyrics? They are tugging at our pant legs and have been since the time of Christ. Peter said he did not have silver or gold to give but he could give Jesus, the bread of life who gives eternal life. We too can give Jesus.

I could have fed more people while I was in India. I had the means but took them for granted and hoarded them. I regret that now. How much more will we regret these things when we are dealing with eternity?

If you could feed the whole world till there was not a hungry soul, would you do it?

Pray: Father, You take care of us, You even forgive our sins. Help us take care of others. Amen.

Thanking God with Spunk

(Sarah Ingwersen)

54

Read: Psalm 100:4

Do you think that when God parted the Red Sea, making enormous walls of water for the Israelites to walk between, they smiled politely and said, "Thanks, Lord," as if He just passed them the peas?

Can you see the shepherds walking calmly home after visiting the baby worshiped by angels?

Would you believe me if I said that after the man born blind received his sight from Jesus, he walked away and continued living as if he'd been able to see his entire life?

If none of these pictures seems quite right, it's because they aren't. In each of these events the people glorified God, celebrating and thanking Him for His majesty, goodness, and graciousness. When I picture it, I see the Israelites jumping up and down, hugging one another, and singing praises and songs of thanksgiving to the Lord. I see the shepherds running excitedly home, telling everyone they meet to thank and praise God because the Savior has been born. I see the blind man washing the clay off his eyes, looking around, relishing the sights surrounding him, and thanking God with joy.

I know these were all extraordinary circumstances that don't seem relevant today. But here's the thing—God didn't have to do what He did. He gave out love for His people, just as He gives you gifts in your life out of love. Everyone has an extraordinary gift—everyone has the gift of salvation because of Jesus' sacrifice on the cross.

So don't just say, "Thanks, God." Remember, salvation is an incredible gift! Go out and celebrate it!

Pray: Dear God, You are amazing! Thank You for all the gifts You have given me, especially the gift of Your Son. Amen.

Disaster Relief

(Sarah Ingwersen)

Read: Psalm 46:1–2

My friend Anna's house flooded on the night of June 20. Her mom watched as the creek in their backyard became a lake. The water reached their patio, filled their basement, and continued rising. It was out of control and out of their hands.

I have to be truthful. I've never stood in the pools of a flood. I've never felt the winds of a tornado. I've never been shaken up by the jolt of an earthquake. I've never actually been threatened by a natural disaster. Wait, let me rephrase that. I've never been threatened by what the world calls a natural disaster.

I have stood in the hospital as doctors wheeled my sister away to the operating room for surgery on her burst appendix. I have felt the winds of a cold wintery day as I walked to my grandma's funeral. I did get shaken up by the jolt of rejection when my best friend told me she didn't want to be friends anymore.

When Anna saw the damage of the flood, a train of emotions took her for a ride—fear, confusion, relief, thankfulness. I'm not going to claim that I know what she was going through—I don't. I've never had to face the challenge of a natural disaster, but I do know this: In times of trouble, when I look to Jesus who died for me, everything turns out okay. God is standing by and He's ready to help us. All we have to do is call on Him and trust Him.

Pray: Dear God, be with me when I face problems in this world. Take away my fear and bring me closer to You with each experience. Amen.

Deadly Accidents

Read: Deuteronomy 8:6

"Hello, Kara. It's Christy. I've got some bad news. My brother Doug was hit by a truck yesterday while he was riding his bike. He was life-flighted to Children's Mercy Hospital. That's where I am now. It's really, really bad. They don't know what is going to happen to him or if he'll make it."

That is the call I woke up to at 8:50 A.M. on Saturday, August 16. Monday, when I talked to Christy, I found out that so much brain damage had occurred from the intense force of the truck that Doug would not live.

His family continued to agonize over him until Tuesday when he went to heaven. They have the peace of knowing that Doug lives with Jesus in heaven because he knew Jesus as the Savior from sin. Doug's family knows that they will see him again. Here on earth their hearts will continue to suffer.

Have you ever thought of a car as a deadly weapon? Not many of us do, but it is. Accidents do happen, even when drivers are cautious and have their attention on the road. However, when drivers are careless, reckless, or under the influence of alcohol or drugs, their car becomes a weapon.

Driving is a privilege, not a right. As Christians we are to obey the laws of God as well as the laws of the land. In fulfilling this duty we obey the driving laws of the state and we obey the law of God that says: Thou shalt not kill.

Pray: God, remind me that when I'm driving, it could be a life or death situation. Help me to remember my responsibilities. Give me patience and guidance. In Jesus' name I pray. Amen.

Dedicated to the memory of Doug Kleinbeck.

Live by God's Design

Read: 1 Corinthians 6:19–20

"You're not going to till *when?*"

"Not until I'm married. Surprised?"

"It's just that …"

"It's just that what?"

"Well, that's a long time! What if you meet the man of your dreams?"

"The man of my dreams will have the same beliefs and values that I do. He will have saved himself also."

"But …"

"I'm not embarrassed about saving sex for marriage—that's God's plan. God created sex to be used within marriage as an expression of total commitment and unity."

"That is so old-fashioned, Kate."

"Laura, times do change, but God's Word doesn't."

That afternoon I continued to explain to Laura why I believed in saving sex for marriage, why it is so important to me. I have promised to be true to God's design for my life and to keep myself sexually pure for the one God has chosen for me.

When sex is saved for marriage, it becomes more than just a physical experience. It is one of the greatest moments of a couple's life—which is what God intended it to be. That moment, on their wedding night, when a husband and wife give themselves to each other for the first time, their two hearts becoming one, united in love, they will confirm the spiritual unity that they share in Jesus Christ. There is only one first time.

Jesus used the picture of the bride and Bridegroom. Jesus is the Bridegroom, the church is His bride. The Bridegroom sacrificed His life on the cross that I might be saved. He loves me that much.

Is it going to be easy to resist all the emotions that I might feel, that might lead me into temptation? No, but as long as I keep my eyes on Jesus the Bridegroom, it will be easier because I know that with God all things are possible.

Pray: God, I ask that You give me courage and strength to resist the temptations I will face. Keep me true to the design You have for my life and for the one You have chosen for me. In Jesus' name. Amen.

Suicide – Help Me Through

(Andrew Kassouf)

Read: Jeremiah 29:11

My life is a living hell! My dad just told me I was a mistake. He's always cutting me down. I guess I'm not living up to his expectations. I can't really tell anyone … they would probably just ignore me. I'm so alone. I feel God won't even listen to me. I've had all I can take!

After crying this to herself for years, she has finally started to believe it. All of this bottled up pain has led to a mental, physical, and spiritual meltdown. She started to picture her funeral. No one was there. She was truly alone. Or so she thought. Although she didn't realize it, God did care, would always listen and be there. God loves her just as He loves all of us—so much that He sent His Son, Jesus, to save us, to pay for our sins. God has a plan for her and He has a plan for you. (See Jeremiah 29:11.)

I walked in just in time. She had the largest knife we owned in her hand. Talk about scared, I was terrified. I love her so much and didn't want to lose her in this way. I had no idea what to do or say, but I personally believe that God is in control and put the right words in my mouth. God saved her so she could fulfill her part in His plan.

If you or a friend are suicidal or are going through tough times, picture God speaking to you while you read this poem.

Confusing Reasons (For the Best)

There are reasons for everything
Though we may not understand
Stay strong
Troubled times are all a part of the
master plan

You've been hit by the pitcher
Of life's many curves
I see it in your face
Rest easy
Protected in my embrace
Don't worry
I will stand by you
Until the very end
Guiding you through the best I can

We are caught crying together
In this great mystery
Called life

Pray: O Lord, thanks for being there for me to turn to in times of need. Show me Your plan for my life and help me through that plan. Amen.

Time Management
for God or for Us?

(Andrew Kassouf)

64

Read: 1 Corinthians 10:31–11:1

What do you find yourself participating in during the course of a week? Probably school, work, sports, and youth group. Whatever it is that we do, we do it to the best of our ability. But do we glorify God or ourselves? Paul wrote in 1 Corinthians 10:31, "Whatever you do, do it all for the glory of God."

Have you allowed Satan to squeeze sinful acts, such as the use of drugs and alcohol, into your schedule? How do you glorify God while sinning against Him? You can't! But you can rearrange your schedule. Fill the time with positive things. Do things with friends from church and always pray about it.

How can I glorify God at school and work? There is always someone special who needs to be reminded of Jesus in times of distress or hear of His love for the first time. So act like Jesus in all situations. (See 1 Corinthians 11:1.)

On the sports field it is very easy to slip and let an obscenity roll off your tongue or let a fist fly. To glorify God try to open the game in prayer, asking God for a fun game whether you win or lose.

When you find yourself wrapped up in worldly things, ask yourself, "Am I glorifying God?" "So whether you eat or drink or whatever you do, do it all for the glory of God" (1 Corinthians 10:31).

Pray: Father God, thank You for sending Your Son. He gave His life so we could have eternal life. When I don't glorify You in my daily actions, forgive me, Lord, and help me live my life serving and glorifying You. Amen.

Death – The Gift

(Andrew Kassouf)

Read: Luke 24:44–49; John 3:16

Have you ever seen young children on Christmas morning? They are in their parents' room at 5:00 A.M. yelling, "Mommy, Daddy, wake up! Santa came last night!" They eventually drag Mom and Dad down to the tree where the long-anticipated gifts await. They aren't yelling, "Mommy, Daddy, wake up! Jesus was born to die today!" Are they? No. But the Son of God was perfectly wrapped in flesh like a perfect Christmas package. How do young children open a gift? They violently tear off the beautiful wrapping paper and inside is a wonderful gift. Long ago, one Friday, we violently tore off Jesus' wrapping. Inside we were given eternal life, the best gift of all. If we believe Jesus died for us, we receive that gift. (See John 3:16.) Oh, and next Christmas, be sure to let the kids know it's not who came down the chimney, but Who came down from heaven that the celebration is all about.

Shadow

Every tree casts a shadow
But none as dark as Yours
You ...
Were mocked for me
Were whipped for me
Were beaten for me
Were killed for me
Were pierced for me

Every tree casts a shadow
But none as bright as Yours
You ...
Were obedient for me
Were sacrificed for me
Were victorious for me
Rose for me

Every tree casts a shadow
But Yours embraces me
You ...
Befriend me
Love me
Cleanse me
Stand with me
Live in me

Thank You, Jesus

Pray: Father, thank You for the ultimate
Christmas gift—Jesus. Thank You for the
forgiveness I have through His death and
resurrection. Amen.

Changing Environment, Changing Friends

Read: Ephesians 6:11

"Hey, Sara, pass the popcorn," Roxanne called, flinging her pillow in Sara's face. The whole gang was just lounging around, making the best of a humid summer's night, watching the movie *Twister* and talking. Everyone sat around basking in the summer's heat until about 12:30 A.M. when they went home. Everyone except William.

William didn't want to walk the 10 blocks home, so he just strolled over to Chris' house. William hadn't seen Chris for a while, in fact, not since he had stopped drinking alcohol.

Chris chuckled as he opened the door, a liquor bottle in his hand, "Well, William, it's been a long time since we've seen you around! I knew you'd come back. We have a rule here: If you want to stay, you have to take a shot." With a little persuasion William broke his vow to his friends, his family, and to himself. He took the shot of alcohol.

If William had gone home or hung out with his other friends, he wouldn't have disappointed the people who meant so much to him. True friends like Sara, Roxanne, and the rest of the gang would never have pressured William into anything he didn't want to do. The negative influence of Chris and certain people changed his perception of his life and his morals.

Is there hope for William? Yes—just as there is hope for all of us if we ask Jesus for forgiveness. He wants us back—He even died on the cross to save us and show us how much He loves us.

When you have temptations like William had, pray this prayer:

Pray: Dear Lord, keep my armor of You so strong that I can keep working with You and for You even when I'm not in a supportive environment. Keep me strong. Help me keep my faith even in the face of adversity. Amen.

Gangs Aren't for Me, Are They?

Read: Matthew 11:28

Peter Nafzger

Gangs? Gangs only exist in places like New York and Los Angeles. I'm not in a gang. In fact, I'd never even heard of any gangs where I grew up.

I've always thought of a gang as a group of people who hang out together and look out for each other. They all have a leader. To get into one, you have to prove how good you are to the other members. When you are in trouble, your gang is where you go for help.

Well, come to think of it, that kind of sounds like my basketball team. I had to try out to prove I could help the team. My teammates and I hang out together and look out for each other. Our captain is our leader. I guess I'm part of that gang.

Then there's my group of friends. There are many people that we don't really get along with so they aren't in our group. I guess that's another gang I'm in.

There is yet another gang that I'm part of. I enjoy hanging out with other members, and we look out for each other. Everyone is invited to join. And there's no price to pay to join—it's been paid by the leader who tells us, "Come to Me, all you who are weary and burdened, and I will give you rest" (Matthew 11:28). He paid for my sins for me because He loves me. If there was ever a reason to join a gang, I'd say eternal life beats them all.

Pray: Dear Lord, help me to see that all the support and love I think I get in the groups I hang out with are nothing compared to being in Your gang. Amen.

Success God's Way

Read: Proverbs 16:3

This was the year. I knew it. My teammates knew it. Our coach knew it. Even our fans knew it. We were ready.

The season flew by with many victories. It was fun, but we had our eyes on the sectional playoff game in the Missouri State Basketball Tournament.

It was the biggest game of my life. I'd never wanted anything more. I prayed that we would win the game. It was a great game. All eyes watched as our team had to make a 30-foot shot at the buzzer. We lost.

How could that happen? God knew how much I wanted that win and how hard I had worked. We were even a Lutheran high school. We prayed the Lord's Prayer before each game. We were committed to the Lord. And God says, "Commit to the LORD in whatever you do, and your plans will succeed" (Proverbs 16:3).

I was committed, but my only view of success was a victory that night. "In his heart a man plans his course, but the LORD determines his steps" (Proverbs 16:9).

I still wish that we had won that game. But it makes me work that much harder on my college team to succeed and has given me a stronger will to do my best. I am also more able to relate to people who suffer disappointments. It makes me think of Jesus' followers during the days after His death—that must have been a huge disappointment for them. But just think of their victory celebration that first Easter—victory Jesus won for all of us.

It took me three years to realize that there was success for me in the loss of that state basketball game. How wonderful to know every day that Jesus has won the only real victory.

Pray: Dear Lord, thank You for the victory You've already won. Give me the strength to commit all that I do to You, and help me to remember that You know what is best for me. Amen.

A Learning Experience

Angie Nichols

Read: Psalm 119:105

I was finally here, an official college student. Independence, new friends ... and, oh yeah, classes. Classes were the aspect of college life that concerned me least. Having made straight A's in high school, I was confident I would do the same in college. Here I was, armed with my 1,000-watt smile and best teacher's pet attitude. I soon came to understand my charms were useless at the university level. As my biology teacher handed me an academic warning, he said, "You aren't making education a priority. You're not reaching your academic potential." His words rang in my ears for days. It took the reality check of academic probation to make me understand that in college there is no tolerance for half-effort.

As I shared my experience with my youth director, he showed me the parallel of what I had faced to what we as Christians face in our faith journey. How often do we fail to make our spiritual education a priority? How many times does our Lord get lost in the commotion of everyday life? Being a Christian is not an easy job. It is a continuous process of learning and growing. Jesus didn't have it easy, either. He came into the world to save sinners, so He went to the cross, He suffered, and He died. He finished the job and in God's eyes, I'm forgiven.

We are told to be "imitators of Christ," and we need instructions on how to fulfill that challenge. God's Word was given to us as a handbook. "Your Word is a lamp to my feet and a light for my path" (Psalm 119:105). Just as we must study to do well in school, we must also study the Bible to equip ourselves for the task of sharing God's love. "And we pray this in order that you may live a life worthy, ... growing in the knowledge of God" (Colossians 1:10).

Pray: Dear Lord, fill me with excitement for learning and growing with You. Help me to be a witness of Your eternal love in all that I do. Amen.

When a Dream Becomes a Nightmare

(Angie Nichols)

Read: Luke 12:6–7

Since the first day of school, he was all she had talked about. His name was Tim. He was basketball captain, youth group president, the "perfect date." As she waited for him to arrive, she envisioned how wonderful the evening would be. Looking back, she realizes how unprepared she was for what lay ahead. The "big date" became her biggest nightmare.

Tim raped my friend that night. He stole something she held close and caused her to question her faith in God. How could she trust a God who would allow a "Christian brother" to take from her so much of what she valued?

After many patient talks with my friend, I helped her realize that during times when we feel the lowest, God's everlasting love flows through us the strongest. I showed her Romans 8:28–39: "And we know that in all things God works for the good of those who love Him. ... For I am convinced ... that [nothing] in all creation, will be able to separate us from the love of God."

Evil things happen in this sinful world. People who seem "good" do terrible things—like raping others, cheating, stealing, or putting Jesus to death. But a lot of "good" came from that last "bad" act—our sins were paid for by a Savior who loves us. When my friend struggled with feelings of unworthiness, I knew it was important for her to understand this and to know that she was a *victim*—what had happened did not lessen her value in God's eyes. We read in Luke 12:6–7: "Are not five sparrows sold for two pennies? Yet not one of them is forgotten by God. Indeed, the very hairs on your head are all numbered. Don't be afraid; you are worth more than many sparrows." That same God will make "good" come from what seems "bad."

Pray: Gracious Lord, be with me when my life seems too difficult to handle on my own. Thank You for the promise that I can do all things through You who give me strength. Amen.

Beyond First Glance

The beginning of school always has that special edge of excitement to it. Even the people who wish summer would last forever take special care to look good for the first day. Why is that?

Since the beginning of time, people have tried to make good first impressions. When you see someone for the first time, it's human nature to pass some sort of judgment about him or her. If someone doesn't dress neatly, he's a slob. When a quiet person studies hard, she gets called a nerd. If he doesn't dress or act like me, I don't think that I'll like him. If she has a different skin color than mine, just forget it.

These, along with others like them, are stereotypes brought about by prejudice. Unfortunately, our sinful world is overrun by such ideas. Problems everywhere have rooted themselves in these trivial things.

I can't believe that God ever intended for people to act this way. Especially not inside the

Christian community. Jesus Himself brought together Greeks, Romans, and Jews to share His saving love. To discredit another is like telling God that you don't like what He's made and redeemed. God loves all that He made—Jesus died for us all. We are to love those Jesus loves.

So try to meet some people that you might normally avoid. The "slob" might be a great guy, just easy going. The "nerd" might just be shy. Possibly best of all you might find a wonderful Christian friend in someone with an entirely different background, culture, or race. Let's say your first impression was correct—you can still follow God's way by setting a Christlike example.

Pray: Dear God, forgive us for those times when we've judged someone unfairly. Help us in the future to see people as You do, not from their appearance, but for who they are. In Christ's name. Amen.

Don't Learn Too Late

Read: Proverbs 13:13

The stars were out that evening, but Tom was too worried about making it home to notice. He'd just dropped off his date when he realized how late it was. Turning onto a larger road, his foot pushed the accelerator nearly to the floor. This would be the third time this week he would be late for curfew.

Tom was never the type to purposely disobey his parents. That's how he'd managed to get his curfew this late, but now he had five minutes left and he was only halfway home. Lately, Tom had begun to worry less about the clock. With two official strikes against him, he was five minutes from being out of action.

Suddenly in his rearview mirror he saw the flashing lights that came along with a siren. Knowing how badly his parents would take this, he pulled over.

Tom sighed as he remembered how his youth director had warned him about these types of things catching up with you. "God can always find a way to make you learn," he'd said. This sure seemed like a good example. Tom thought about his parents—they really only wanted what was best for him, just as God wants what is best for us. That's why He gave His only Son to die for us—so we might be His forgiven sons and daughters. Tom decided that honoring your father and mother included making curfew. He made up his mind to start planning his evenings better.

Then, with a wail and a blur of color, the cop sped by. On his way somewhere else. Tom was relieved and continued home, only slower. His parents weren't awake when he arrived 10 minutes late, but Dad had left a note: "Proverbs 13:13."

Pray: Dear God, forgive me when I disobey You and my parents. Help me so I don't learn too late about listening to my parents' concerns about curfew. Help me to see where my parents are coming from and to realize it is in my best interest not only to obey but to respect them as well. In Christ's name. Amen.

Another Christian Chameleon

(Philip J. Potyondy

Read: 2 Corinthians 6:14–18

"Good morning, Mr. Peterson!"

"Good morning, Cindy. How was your week?"

"Just fine. Oh, hi, Jake! How's the knee? I've been praying for you."

"Thanks, Cindy, it feels better. The doctor says I should be off my crutches by the end of the week."

"That's great to hear. See ya."

It's just an average Sunday for Cindy. First she greets people before church starts. Then she goes to worship. After worship she helps with Sunday school classes. Finally she tops the morning off by hanging out with kids her age from her church at a local restaurant.

She is a fun person to have around, and her friends appreciate her Christian attitude toward life. But she isn't always this way.

"Hey, Cindy! Are you coming to the party tonight to get drunk?"

"Wouldn't miss it for the world."

This is another average ritual for Cindy. Only this time it's Friday night. After work Cindy usually gets invited to a party. She knows that there are going to be a lot of things there she shouldn't mess with such as getting drunk, doing drugs, and possibly sex, but she usually goes anyway.

After she's under the influence of not only chemicals but the people who are there, she starts saying and doing things she usually wouldn't say or do.

Then she's back to Sunday morning:

"Good morning, Mrs. Tillmen!"

"Good morning, Cindy. How was your week?"

"Just great! Hey, Julie, it sure is good to see you here at church. How's it going?"

After less then 48 hours she seems like a totally different person. Some might call her a hypocrite.

What kind of environment do you surround yourself with? And how does it affect the way you act? Think about it.

Pray: Father God, thank You for being an awesome God. Lord, grant me wisdom so I may make the right decision about who I surround myself with. Forgive me for Jesus' sake for all the times I have not made decisions as I should. Remind me to turn to You for the strength to do what I know is right. Amen.

Called to Be Witnesses

(Heather Scheiwe

Read: Jeremiah 1:4–9

Most kids have gotten the impression from adults that we're not very important, that we're a nuisance to society. We don't really have anything to offer because we're young. We don't have the experience to be intelligent speakers. Well, God sees us differently. (See 1 Timothy 4:12.) We have what it takes to be fruitful witnesses to our friends. Even though it doesn't seem cool, God gives us situations to show our friends His amazing love without being pushy.

Imagine a watering can. A gardener fills the can through a faucet, watching carefully until the water level reaches the top. Then the gardener tenderly carries the can outside where he proceeds to water the dry, wilting flowers. He repeats this procedure until all the plants have been thoroughly watered.

This is how God uses us to witness to our friends. We are called to Christ, the Gardener, through the waters of Holy Baptism.

He continues to fill us with His blessings and love. Then when we're full, we share the Gospel with others.

I challenge you to be a vessel for God, carrying His love and guidance with you always. Share it with your friends through little things: declining when they ask you to do something that's wrong, being there when they need to talk, wearing a cross and telling them that it is a symbol reminding us that Jesus our Savior died for us and forgives us, and simply praying for them. Don't worry if you don't see results right away. Remember that God will use you to water thirsty seeds. It may take years for them to grow, or it may be days. That's all in God's hands. All we can do is be there when the Gardener wants to use us.

Pray: Dearest Jesus, You have called me to be a witness to my friends. Help me to get over my timidity, and make me a bold witness for You. I want so badly to reach my friends who don't yet know You. Help me water them with Your astounding love, and let them grow closer to the Son. Amen.

Defeating Evil

Read: Ephesians 6:10-18

The devil. His tricks are dirty. He plays with your mind. He wants to take control. He'll do anything to get hold of your soul and drag it down with him and his angels. It's a scary thought to know that there's a force out there that can literally kill you inside and out. He works through many things to make you believe he's right: friends, school, entertainment. One powerful shape Satan comes in is cults.

A cult seems like such a crock, something that only wackos get involved with. In fact, the majority of followers in a cult are everyday people who fall under the grasp of the devil's schemes. You see, he twists the truth to make it tempting. Remember when he used the Word of God to try to persuade Jesus to jump off the temple? (See Matthew 4:5-7.) He twisted it around so it sounded like the right thing to do. The devil tried every trick to get Jesus to give up His work as the Savior—suffering and dying on the cross to pay for our sins. But Jesus knew what was right. He knew the reason He was in the world was to defeat death and the devil and He stood firm in His convictions.

We're all called to be like Jesus. He says we'll be able to discern between good and evil by studying His Word. We can "put on the full armor of God" to protect us from the tricks the devil plays. Cults can't get to us when we have God on our side. He's like a giant warrior standing by to fight with us in the battles of this world. With truth, righteousness, the Gospel, peace, faith, salvation, and the Holy Spirit working for us, we can stand firm when the devil decides to try his dirty tricks on us. We will win!

Pray: Lord, help me to stand firm and know what's right in Your sight. The devil has put everything in my way: cults, evil thoughts, temptation. Be with me as we fight for what is right. Amen.

ƒƒƒƒ

Making Noise

Heather Scheiwe

Read: Psalm 33

My friend and I, both involved in musical groups at school, were asked to share our love of music with the first- through third-grade classes at our church. We were a little wary at first but were soon delighted to sing with them. There was one girl in class who had a special impact on me. She was normally quiet, but when she sang, it was with all her might. Most little kids have fairly decent voices, missing a few pitches occasionally. This girl, however, never hit the right note. She would sing louder than any of the other kids, sometimes getting strange looks, but she sang with a smile on her face. She seemed like an angel in a heavenly choir.

Why was this little girl so different from the rest? She sang from her heart. That's what God calls us to do: praise Him with whatever talents we have. He doesn't want us competing with one another for the position of best singer or most talented baseball player. God doesn't care how many people we beat. He cares that we praise Him in all things. The little girl loved the Lord so much that it didn't matter if she couldn't sing a note. The Bible says to make a *joyful* noise to the Lord, not a beautiful one. And we have so much to praise God for. After all, He loved us so much, He died for us and made us clean. That's certainly reason to sing!

So whatever talents you have—music, theater, art, sports, or even mathematics—praise God fully with them. He loves to see His children praising Him with all their hearts. It's hard not to praise God after all the wonderful things He's done for us.

Pray: Lord, help me today to praise You fully with whatever I do. You've done so much for me that sometimes I get carried away with my talents and turn them into a competition. Help me get over my competitive spirit and focus on glorifying Your name. Amen.

Good Times

Read: Psalm 16:11

All of us have had those really bummer days where nothing seems to go right. We wake up late, can't eat breakfast, miss our ride, are tardy to class, and forget our homework assignments. By the end of the day, you just want to scream. Instead, we can lean on God to get us through. Luckily, those kinds of days only come once in a while for most of us. The rest of the time, life is good, and we're happy to be living. So how does God work in us then?

First of all, when you're happy on the inside, it usually shows on the outside. Chances are someone walking down the hallway is having one of those not-so-good days. Just smile. It could be one of the most helpful things for the other person. He is probably down on himself and thinking, "Hey, maybe someone out there really does care." God even says, "A cheerful look brings joy to the heart" (Proverbs 15:30). *God* brings joy to our hearts. He paid for our sins by dying and rising again, so we are alive in Him. That gives me great joy! We can share the joy in our hearts with others who definitely need the joy Christ provides.

Most important, praise God for His goodness in your life. It seems that in good times you notice God's bountiful blessings more. Use that time to thank Him for all He's done. Here's a good verse to memorize and think about when you're feeling great: "Be joyful always; pray continually; give thanks in all circumstances, for this is God's will for you in Christ Jesus" (1 Thessalonians 5:16–18).

Pray: Thank You, heavenly Father, for all Your blessings in my life. Help me to praise You in good times and share Your amazing love with others. I'm so happy You gave me life! Amen.

Living with Limits

Kristen Smith

Read: Proverbs 29:18

"Can Erin and I go out with some friends after the game?" I thought it seemed like a simple question. What could go wrong? Then came the answer.

"What time will you be home?" Uh-oh.

"Wellll, Erin has to be in by midnight, so it'll be before that."

Maybe that would get me off the hook.

"We didn't set your curfew at midnight. You'd better be in by 11:30 tonight so Erin can be in by 12:00 A.M. But you will be in before that." Great, so now I've got to be in by 11:29.

"And be careful, you know teenage drivers." When I thought it couldn't get any worse, Dad sounds like an insurance guy. This is so unfair.

From a teenager's point of view, things in life don't always seem fair, especially rules. And sometimes they aren't fair. But many times our parents actually do speak from a voice of experience that we are still clueless about. Although we don't always understand our parent's reasoning, God promises to bless us by our obedience to them. Not obedience part of the time, or when we feel like it, but all the time. And that includes curfews.

"Where there is no revelation, the people cast off restraint; but blessed is he who keeps the law" (Proverbs 29:18).

I did, by the way, get home at 11:20.

Pray: Heavenly Father, help me to remember that my parents set rules and curfews to keep me from harm. Give me the patience and wisdom to follow their advice and rules. When I break Your rules and theirs, forgive me for the sake of Jesus who died for me. In Jesus' name. Amen.

Three Isn't Always a Crowd

(Kristen Smith)

Read: 2 Thessalonians 3:5

What was the big deal? So what if I wasn't comfortable taking my boyfriend to church with me. Was that so bad? But I couldn't forget the conversation that I'd had with my youth director that evening at youth group.

"What's this I hear that you're dating some guy pretty seriously?" she'd asked.

"I wouldn't say *serious*, just *dating*. And it's Steve, not some guy. Why?"

"You must be hiding him from us."

"I guess it just didn't seem important."

"Is there more to it than that?"

"What?!"

"Are you afraid of bringing him to church? Afraid that maybe he'll think you're a *Jesus freak*?"

The more I went over her words, the more I realized she was right. Steve and I had never discussed religion. He knew I was a Christian, and he'd seen me pray before. But was that enough? Should I have been involving him in my church life too? Was I just scared of what he'd think of me? I knew it was now or never. I called Steve that night and asked him to go to church with me Sunday morning. Surprised that I'd asked, he agreed.

That Sunday, my pastor preached on the third chapter of Thessalonians: "May the Lord direct your hearts into God's love and Christ's perseverance" (3:5). Was I trying to hide my God? I thought that a relationship was only between two people. But I had left out the most important thing in the relationship—my Savior, who gave His life for me, who loves me, and who is always ready to forgive when I come to Him.

Involve God in *all* your relationships.

Pray: Almighty Father, You created love and relationships. Let me always keep You as the focus in all my relationships. Amen.

Special Friend

(Melissa Strelow)

Read: Proverbs 18:24

Recently, I was going through a very difficult time. I was in a big fight with my best friend and we hadn't spoken to each other in awhile. I found comfort, once again, in God's Word: "There is a friend who sticks closer than a brother" (Proverbs 18:24). This verse says to me that Jesus will stay by my side no matter what. He will always be my friend.

A few years ago, I wrote this poem about a special friend:

> My special friend is always there,
> Lending an ear or a shoulder to cry on.
> My special friend will always be with me
> along that long, long road of life.
>
> My special friend will always care
> And will never leave my side.
> No matter what I do or where I go,
> My special friend will be my lifelong
> guide.
>
> Through times of pain and struggle,
> My special friend will be with me.

Holding my hand and walking by my side,
Helping me through any problem there
may be.

I can go to my special friend with any
problem I may have.
No matter what the time or the place.
Always near me, never far away,
Yet I have never seen my friend's face.

My friend gave up His life for me,
He gave the ultimate sacrifice.
Someday I will see
Him in His heavenly home, my friend,
Jesus Christ.

God is there for you all the time, and He
will listen to all your problems. He is the Friend
that will always be true.

Pray: Heavenly Father, thank You for always
being there and caring for me, for loving
me and forgiving me. Help me try to be a
better friend, and remind me that You are
always there no matter what I may be
going through. In Your name. Amen.

Train Hard – Don't Cheat

Melissa Strelow

Read: 2 Timothy 2:5;
1 Corinthians 9:25

Sports are important to many teenagers, and many take them very seriously. But when does winning become too big a price to pay?

It's too far when cheating comes into the picture. The old saying *Cheaters never prosper* is true according to 2 Timothy 2:5: "Similarly, if anyone competes as an athlete, he does not receive the victor's crown unless he competes according to the rules." But, you think, if I break the rules a few times, is it really going to hurt? Maybe cheating once to win an important game won't hurt, but will it be okay the next time?

Instead of taking the easy way out, train hard and win using your abilities. What you do on the court can impact your daily life. If you cheat to win in sports, you may start cheating to win in life. "Everyone who competes in the games goes into strict training. They do it to get a crown that will not last; but we do it to get a crown that will last forever" (1 Corinthians 9:25). This verse talks about strict training through prayer and reading the Bible. Physical training is important but not as important as training to be strong in your faith. When you have Jesus by your side, He helps you do everything. With His help, cheating becomes unnecessary. So, train hard both spiritually and physically. Do this, and you will be a winner no matter what happens in the game.

Pray: Dear Lord, help me resist the temptation to cheat. I know I have broken Your rules—forgive me for the sake of Jesus who died for me. Help me train hard with Your Spirit to get my faith in shape along with my body. Amen.

My Parents' Expectations

Brett Thurman

Read: Ephesians 6:1–4

My parents have always told me that no matter what I do, they will always love me. It hadn't occurred to me until recently exactly what that entailed. Sure, there are some things that they wish I would do, but they have always accepted me for who I am and not for whom they expected me to be. I think that their unconditional love for me is the closest thing to Christ's love that a human can experience.

Just think about what that statement means. "We will always love you no matter what you do." Does that sound familiar? Do the words *forgiveness* and *grace* come to mind? Christ's love for us is evident in all aspects of our lives, especially in our parents' love for us. I know that not everyone's parents show the same kind of love and all parents aren't Christians. But whether they find ways to show it or not, parents, no matter who they are, have a love for their children that almost surpasses understanding. Everybody shows it differently, and some don't show it at all, but parents have an inborn love for their children. I believe this is another one of God's great blessings to help us along in our daily struggles. So if you stay in God's light and strive to live in Christ, I'm sure that whatever you may do, you will meet your parents' expectations.

Pray: Lord, help us to follow Your will in all that we do. Help us to please and honor our parents in our love for You. Thank You for sending Jesus to die for us. Amen.

Yes,

...but We Don't Practice

Read: Matthew 11:28-30

(Brett Thurman)

"Yes, my family is Christian, but we don't practice." This was the answer I received when my friend and I started talking about religion and I asked if he belonged to a church. By this response he meant that he didn't attend any church.

As we talked some more, he said he wasn't sure if he believed in Christ because he had never "felt" Him in his life. He told me that he didn't feel any comfort when he thought of his Savior, that he was having some really tough times at school, and that Christ didn't seem to be taking any of the pressures off. He didn't understand that Jesus did much more than take the pressure off—He *bore* the pressure of our sins when He went to the cross to save us. If He can stand the pressure of our sins, He can help us through whatever we're going through.

When I got home, I started thinking of what I could tell my friend. Then I realized that there was a direct link between his feelings about Christ and his church life. In Matthew 11:28–30, Christ tells us that if we come to Him, He will give us rest. Belonging to Christ isn't meant to be something that makes life harder, it's meant to make life easier.

I will admit that you don't have to go to church to feel Christ's love and helping hand. He's with you all the time, especially when life is really tough. But He has given us the gift of fellowship. One of the reasons Christ instituted the church was that He knew we would need friends who believed the same as we do—friends who could offer comfort in a time of trouble, friends faithful to Christ.

Next time you feel run down or troubled, talk about it with Christ, and also your pastor, or a close Christian friend. You can take comfort in the fact that Christ is there, always.

Pray: Lord, help me to come to You with my troubles so You can give me strength to endure. Amen.

The Only True Protection

Brett Thurman

Read: Titus 2:11–12

"The only true protection is abstinence." Sure, we've all heard pastors, teachers, and parents telling us how to handle sex before marriage. For them the answer is simple, "Just say no!" and we have all thought the same thing, "Easy for you to say."

Why is everyone always publicizing safe sex? The biggest reason is sexually transmitted diseases. When I was asked to write this devotion, I immediately felt defeated. Here they were, asking me to write about something some parents are scared to even think of. And to top it off, I realized that they had gotten me, a teenager, to tell all my peers that sex should wait for marriage. I sort of felt like Moses, "Why would they listen to me?"

So this is how I see it: Yes, intercourse before marriage is a sin and, yes, it can have severe consequences. But wait, it's not just us against the pressures of the world. Do you really think God expects us to go it alone? He is with us. He is here to help, guide, and comfort us.

If you were to ask your pastor for guidance in this matter, one thing he may tell you is to read your Bible and look for support there. Well, that's just fine, but I prefer a more direct approach. Before and after every date, just take a few seconds to ask God to stay by your side. Just 30 seconds—that's not too long. Just ask Him to help you remember His plan for you. Because, in the end, the only true protection is God.

Pray: Lord, stay with me and guide me when I may go astray. Help me to always remember that You love me so much that You died for me. Thank You for loving and forgiving me. Amen.

Life after Death

(Jason Timm)

Read: Psalm 16:10–11

A few months ago I had a relative pass away. This was the first funeral that I remember attending. I felt sad for the rest of the family, but I was happy in a way because I knew that he was in heaven enjoying eternal life with our Lord.

When a loved one dies, we feel grieved that he or she is not with us any longer. We sometimes wish that death didn't have to happen at all. One reaction to death is that we can become angry with God and have to be reminded that our loved one is free of sin and all suffering. With faith in Christ we will see him or her again in heaven.

Since the funeral I have been trying to look at death with a different perspective. It is challenging, but I am finding it easier to be at peace with God about death and eternal life. Friends say they are sorry about the death, but later I think, "Sorry for what? He's in heaven with our Lord. I hope he's having a good time."

Nothing can prepare us for death, but God's Word helps us through it. At times like these we need someone to comfort us. Through His death and resurrection, Christ paid the penalty for our sins. He'll give us hope and strength to endure. Remember, God will help you in all times of trouble.

Pray: Dear Father in heaven, be with us always and guide us especially in hard times when we might fall away. Remind us that our loved ones are with You in heaven and that we will see them again someday. We pray this in Your name. Amen.

Lost in a World of Success

Read: Luke 12:13–21

(Jason Timm

This passage isn't saying that if we have an abundance of possessions, God will take our lives. It is saying that we should not put faith in material things for a long, happy, and secure life. We need to keep faith in our Lord. Sometimes we get caught up in our own success and forget about God. If we no longer have faith in God, our possessions are useless. Without God, wouldn't we feel something missing in our lives? Some families get so caught up in life that they don't think about God, and things can fall apart.

Remember the Bible story of the man with a great abundance of crops? He stored it all, thinking that it would last him a long time. That night, God came and took his life. The man put his faith in his crops to support him, not God. His trust in money got him nowhere. His wealth couldn't help him or support him once he died. He forgot that the greatest success is eternal life that Jesus earned for us when He died on the cross.

The same thing happens today. You try to get the most you can and don't think about what might happen. You could lose it all overnight. Success isn't a bad thing if you know where your priorities lie. God can help us with our successes and our failures.

Keep God first. He will be with you always. Don't lose sight of Him. Keep the faith.

Pray: Lord, while some are more successful than others, help us all to remember You. If we get lost in our own worlds of success, guide us to do the right thing in whatever we do and not to stray from the path to Your kingdom. Amen.

Mind Your Own Business

Read: Proverbs 16:28

"What do you think about the way Cassandra and Marcus are acting?"

All I had to say was "It's none of my business." However, I chose to make it my business. So I said, "I think it's awful. And you know what, I bet ..." Then I proceeded to tell everyone what I thought was going on between Cassandra and Marcus.

After we had that conversation, I didn't feel guilty about talking behind my friends' backs. We were just talking like we always did. In fact, I forgot all about the conversation until the phone rang two nights later. It was Cassandra.

It seems someone had told Cassandra about the conversation. Cassandra wanted to know if I had said those things. I told her the truth and then she told me the real story. Boy, did I feel stupid! I apologized and Cassandra forgave me, but our friendship would never be the same.

We weren't "just talking" that day. We were gossiping. Not only did it hurt Cassandra and Marcus, it hurt us too. Because Cassandra found out her "friends" were gossiping about her, she would never trust us in the same way again. Gossip hurts people—even destroys them—and it doesn't show love. But Jesus died for us all and loves us all—even the people we hurt with our gossip.

Now, whenever I feel the urge to gossip, I just remember how close Cassandra and I once were, and I feel sad that we're not that close anymore. Basically, I think of what the consequences could be if I don't mind my own business. And I remember what Jesus did on the cross—for me, for Cassandra, for everyone.

Pray: God, thank You for blessing me in so many ways, especially through all my friends. Help me to treat my friends just like Jesus, our best Friend, treats us. In Your name. Amen.

It's Yours — Guaranteed

Read: Ephesians 3:17b–19

(Amy Wood

"Fourteen- and fifteen-year-old girls who want to get pregnant and have a baby"—on the next *Jerry Springer Show.*

Every summer I usually spend my days catching up on soap operas and I read at night. However, this summer I had a job, so at night I watched TV. Little did I know I would become hooked on talk shows.

Some of the talk shows were about "serious" issues, while others had outrageous topics. Somehow, I enjoyed the outrageous topics the most. While channel surfing I came across a serious topic I decided to watch. It was about teenage girls who wanted to have babies.

As I listened to each of the girls tell their story, it occurred to me that they must not know God very well. When asked why, the girls all responded with the same answer. They wanted someone who would love them, guaranteed.

I would have never thought of "feeling unloved" as a reason to have a baby. Yet, with these six girls, that was the case.

After watching the show, I wished I could let them know they *are* loved. God loves them so much that He sent His one and only Son to die on the cross for them. The love that God has for us is so real and deep that it's all we need, and it's guaranteed.

Pray: God, thank You for loving us so deep and wide that You sent Your one and only Son to die on the cross for our sins. Help us to remember that we are loved and to love one another in the same way. In Your name. Amen.

A Gnawing Hunger

Read: John 6:48–50

(J. Bruhl)

I pushed back from the table, stuffed with my mom's roast and mashed potatoes. I excused myself and plopped down on the couch to watch football. As the TV came on, I was greeted by a commercial, begging for support to help starving children. With a tinge of guilt, I changed the channel and tuned into football. I tried to concentrate on the game but was stuck with the faces of the starving children. I flipped back to the commercial in time to see it fade out on a little girl's face, emaciated and streaked with tears. Disturbed, I went down to my room and lay on my bed. My stomach wrestled with dinner.

The world is hungry. We see it in commercials and on the news. Personally I have seen it face to face, on a mission trip to West Africa. It's a horrifying sight. There are millions around the world whose bodies are weak and aching because of the lack of food, their stomachs gnawing constantly for sustenance. We can all see the effects of this hunger.

People are starving everywhere we go. They are also hungering for something to fill an aching hole that lingers in their heart. We as Christians have the bread of life that can fill this void. His name is Jesus—He loves us, died for us, and forgives us. People all around us are dying spiritually while we sit next to them, holding the fruit that can ease their pain. Jesus calls to the starving in John 6:35: "I am the bread of life. He who comes to Me will never go hungry." We have the Good News that can nourish a starving world.

Yet, we cannot fail to neglect the physical suffering of God's created. We can feed the hungry with food, opening their hearts to listen to the message of salvation, filling their stomachs and hearts with the joy of contentment. Through our help at home, hundreds around the world can be saved.

Pray: Dear Lord and Giver of life, we thank You so much for all the wonderful gifts You have given us. We pray that we would remember every day how blessed we are. We also pray that You would give us the opportunity and courage to share Your Good News with a starving world. Bless us in the fulfillment of Your Great Commission and in our service to others. In Your name we pray. Amen.

Cross-Shaped Hole

"You have no idea!"

"You're right. I have no idea. How could someone like you get into drugs? You have everything: a good family, nice clothes, a car, everything."

"You don't understand. When I'm tripping, everything feels great. There are no problems, no pain. All I know is that every day something is missing, there is just a hole somewhere. But when I'm high, none of that matters. It's all good."

There was a song that was popular a couple of years ago that says, "A circle can't fit where a square should be." Nothing could better explain the problem with drugs. Yes, people do drugs because of peer pressure, and even sometimes because they are looking for fun and excitement. But the problem comes *after* the high, when they come crashing back down to reality. The emptiness they felt before is still

J. Bruhl

116

there. An emptiness that can only be filled with the blood of the cross.

When we are conceived and born into sin, we enter the world with a piece missing from our heart. People spend entire lifetimes trying to fill this void. Cars, wealth, sex, adrenaline, and drugs are just some of the pieces that people try to shove into the cross-shaped hole that lies inside them. Drugs, with all their promise of adventure and fun, lead only to frustration and despair. You cannot fit a syringe where a cross should be.

The longing that people are trying to fill with drugs can only be healed with the blood of Jesus' sacrifice. The story of Christ's death and resurrection is the only thing that can bring true fulfillment to a person's life.

Pray: Dear Lord, open our eyes to those around us who are hurting. Shine Your light through us so we may lead others to You. Fill our hearts daily with Your love, and reassure us of Your salvation. Do not let our hearts wander. Keep our eyes focused on You. Amen.

Danger in the Air

Read: Mark 4:39-41

During my freshman year in high school, some of my classmates from school and I had traveled to a state arts and academic competition in Austin, Texas. The weather was threatening. When we arrived, we were a little scared. We had reason to be, for we soon found out a tornado was moving through the area. We were in danger. The scariest part of the whole thing was that we were stuck in a building made of glass. As I looked around, I realized that most of the people were just talking, perhaps to keep from thinking of the worst.

Later that night, after the storm and tornado had passed by, I had time to reflect on what had happened. The scripture verse that came to mind was Luke 12:22-23, "Do not worry about your life, what you will eat; or about your body, what you will wear." In reality I had no reason to fear. I have a God who promised, "Never will I leave you; never will I forsake you" (Hebrews

13:5). Whether surrounded by friends or when I'm by myself, I can take courage in that.

Pray: Father, thank You for protecting me always—from dangers in life and from sin and death. I praise You for the salvation You give me through the death and resurrection of Your Son, Jesus. In His name. Amen.

Volley What?

Read: Psalm 145:10–12

It was my first day at a new school. I didn't know anyone, and I felt lost in the endless hallways. The day finally ended, and I was glad. But now it was time for me to try out for the volleyball team. I had never played a team sport before, and I was really nervous—especially since I wasn't a very good volleyball player. When I arrived at practice in the gym, I found myself surrounded by girls who could volley the ball without missing.

I was sure I wouldn't make the team. Then I noticed a group of girls off to one side that couldn't even keep the ball in the air. I felt much better and walked over to join them. I introduced myself and told them I was a beginning volleyball player and didn't expect to make the cut. They laughed and said that they probably weren't any better off than I.

While we were warming up, we got to talking about religion and God. I told them I was a Lutheran. They either said that they were Christian or they really didn't believe in God.

Sometimes I question if God really is there watching out for me and guiding me to make right decisions. I understood how these girls felt. The coach arrived, and we had to start practice. We could finish the conversation later. I wished everyone good luck, and I thought to myself, I will pray for them.

As it turned out, I became a better player after a little practice and a lot of encouragement. By the middle of the season, I had made quite a few friends, and some of them were visiting my church. I'm still trying to get them to join. Maybe with a few more prayers, invitations, and a little practice, they will change their minds.

You know, I don't feel new anymore. I've learned to get around the school without being late for class, I've made lots of friends, and I can even play volleyball. But most important, I've learned that God can use me to help others know Him. All I have to do is tell them about the great friend I have in Jesus who loves me, forgives me, and died for me.

Pray: Holy God, You are present in the hallways and classrooms of my school. Keep them safe places where friendships can be made, new things learned, and students can grow. Make my school a place where Your name can be shared and where those who do not know You may learn about You. In Your name. Amen.

Music

How many times have your parents asked you why you like a certain song? I know my father has said that a billion times. And I always say, "Just because." Or, when I'm singing a song, he'll ask me, "Erin, how many hymns have you memorized?" After that, I'll sing "Amazing Grace" or his personal favorite, "Brothers and Sisters." Many of the odd people to whom we refer as parents or legal guardians think *music* affects us, to which we reply in a *clueless* kind of way, "whatever" or "as if." And we're right, music doesn't, lyrics do. And it isn't only us, it's society as well.

My mom always says that if I'm ever being followed I should belt out "Rock of Ages" off-key. She's right, that will make me look insane. But let's say I start singing a song such as "Red Light Special." Then I'll look easy and may give wrong signals. Sure, music can be fun to dance to, and I love to dance. But even I find a lot of the songs I like to dance to are quite tasteless and go against what I believe is right. I'm not going to change my life because of the words. When I buy a CD, I think that my money is supporting that artist's lifestyle.

So what do you do? Stop listening to the "in" music? Quit going to dances? No, that would stink! But remember that there are groups out there that sound good and are Christian. (Ever listen to Newsboys? Jars of Clay? Kurt Franklin?) Keep in mind that God loves to be praised. Did you know that Jesus sang with the disciples the night before He was crucified? He had just instituted the Lord's Supper where He gives us His body and blood, shed on the cross for our sins. When Jesus sang with the disciples, it was most likely a psalm. Think of Jesus singing when you're deciding what music to listen to. And sing your heart out in church on Sunday and see just how many hymns you can memorize.

Pray: Dear heavenly Father, help us to remember to praise You through our actions and the words in the music we listen to. Be with us today and hold us in Your hands for the rest of our lives. Amen.

Stay in the Game

Read: 1 Chronicles 28:20

Erin Dittmer

The ball crossed in front of the goal. BANG! I slapped the ball in and scored! What a rush! What a feeling! I looked around to see if my mom was as excited as I was. I looked twice. I didn't see her anywhere. My heart dropped a little, but my coach yelled to stay in the game. We hadn't won yet. After the game, I saw my mom walking toward the field. She had missed my goal but still commended me on my effort and hard work. My disappointment didn't compare to hers. She felt horrible for missing it.

Life is kind of like field hockey. It can be frustrating to watch and to play. There are times that I have the rush and the exhilarating feelings, and there are times that I can be let down. No day, or game, is perfect but when something does go wrong, God encourages me to stay in the game. He may not say it to me personally, through a cloud or something, but I know that He is sending this good news to me every day. Whether it's through my coach, my friends, my family, or my teachers, I am told to "hang in there." Jesus "stayed in the game" when He was on the cross.

It looked like He was losing but He wasn't. When He said, "It is finished," He won. He had paid for our sins and conquered death and the devil. He won so we could win.

So what if you are bummed about something? You're really upset and nobody seems to be inspiring you? Then you have to depend on God. Open your Bible and read a verse about how God got people through life's many dilemmas and heartaches. A good verse to read is 1 Chronicles 28:20.

Here they were talking about a temple, but it still fits our lives. Think of the temple as our life. Just as they went through the hardships of building the temple, we need to be constantly built up when life's little pains tear us down. Take David's advice and be strong. God is with you and is like your coach. He won't let you stop until He's done with you.

So next time you don't do so well on a test or miss the winning basket, don't get discouraged. Life will have disappointments and penalty shots, glorious moments and victories. The game won't end because the coach won't let you quit.

Pray: Lord, be with us as we play the game of life. Help us to understand and learn from the problems we will face. Remind us that You are our coach and that we need to keep our ears open to hear Your game plan. Stay in our minds as we celebrate the victories that only You can help us achieve. Amen.

Do You Know Where We Are?

Read: Matthew 28:20

(Martha Hiller

"Do you know where we are?" I asked my sister.

"Of course I do. We're on our way to Jason's house," was her confident response. "Trust me. I have a great sense of direction."

An hour had passed, and I knew we were going the wrong way, but I didn't want to say anything to my sister. I knew she was already nervous. About 20 minutes later, we knew for sure we were driving in the wrong direction. My sister was very frustrated—you could tell by the look in her eyes. We pulled into a shopping center parking lot to call home.

"Pass me the phone, Martha," she said. I responded rather quickly, "I don't have it. I thought you had it." This situation was not going to get any better. I tried to sound confident as I assured her that I had enough quarters to cover the cost of using the pay phone.

I tried to convince her to go home, but she was determined that she could do it. We called home, got new directions, and started off once again. An hour later, we still had not found Jason's house. I knew we should stop, but my sister wanted to keep going just a little further.

It was almost an hour later before we had a chance to stop. We looked for a sign to indicate where we were and saw one for Waldorf. We didn't know where Waldorf was, but we knew it was past our destination. We had to face the fact that we were truly lost. I told my sister we should take a deep breath and pray. We thanked God for keeping us safe this far and asked Him to watch over us and make sure we had a safe journey home. We called our parents to ask them for help. They couldn't understand how we got so far away from where we were supposed to be. My sister was scared and in tears. I assured her that everything would work out. God was by our side.

We got directions we hoped would take us home. We thought we were on the right track when we saw the signs for Washington. We thought it would be funny if we saw the Washington Monument. And the next thing we saw *was* the Washington Monument.

My sister started to sob. I knew God was watching over us and things would turn out okay. We found a pay phone and called our parents. By the grace of God, our next-door neighbor's son, who worked in Washington, knew exactly where we were.

My sister and I sat in the car, awaiting our parents' arrival, thanking God for keeping us safe throughout what seemed like an endless journey. We arrived home safely and prayed once again to say thanks.

Sometimes I feel lost even when I'm not riding with my sister. But then I think about Jesus' parable of the lost sheep—I know what that sheep felt like. But Jesus *found* the lost sheep. And Jesus, the Good Shepherd, died for His "sheep" so we could be found, loved, forgiven, restored, and brought back safely into God's family. I'm glad that I have a God who doesn't lose sight of me, and who promises to be with me always.

Pray: Heavenly Father, thank You for making me Yours and for loving me so much that You always know where I am. Keep me safe in Your presence during all the days and activities of my life. And Lord, while I'm out driving, watch over me and all those other drivers who just might be as lost as I was. In Your name. Amen.